D0551533

Landforms

Caves

Cassie Mayer

 www.heinemann.co.uk/library
Visit our website to find out more information about **Heinemann Library** books.

To order:
☎ Phone 44 (0) 1865 888066
▤ Send a fax to 44 (0) 1865 314091
▢ Visit the Heinemann Bookshop at www.heinemann.co.uk/library to browse our catalogue and order online.

First published in Great Britain by Heinemann Library, Halley Court, Jordan Hill, Oxford OX2 8EJ, part of Harcourt Education. Heinemann is a registered trademark of Harcourt Education Ltd.

Editorial: Tracey Crawford, Cassie Mayer, Dan Nunn, and Sarah Chappelow
Design: Jo Hinton-Malivoire
Picture Research: Ruth Blair
Production: Duncan Gilbert

Originated by Chroma Graphics (Overseas) Pte. Ltd
Printed and bound in China by South China Printing Company

10 digit ISBN 0 431 18230 2
13 digit ISBN 978 0 431 18230 8

11 10 09 08 07
10 9 8 7 6 5 4 3 2 1

British Library Cataloguing in Publication Data
Mayer, Cassie
  Caves. - (Landforms)
  1.Caves - Juvenile literature
  I.Title
  551.4'47
A full catalogue record for this book is available from the British Library.

Acknowledgements
The publishers would like to thank the following for permission to reproduce photographs: Alamy pp. **6** (Chris Howes/Wild Places Photography), **11** (Chris Howes/Wild Places Photography), **22** (Simon Colmer and Abby Rex); Corel Professional Photos p. **13** (all); Corbis pp. **4** (river, Pat O'Hara; mountain, Royalty Free; volcano, Galen Rowell; island, George Steinmetz), **5** (Layne Kennedy), **7** (Tim Wright), **10** (Bob Krist), **12** (Richard T. Nowitz), **14** (P. van Gaalen/zefa), **15** (Tom Bean), **17** (David Muench), **18** (Eric and David Hosking), **19** (Wolfgang Kaehler), **20** (Danny Lehman), **21** (Annie Griffiths Belt), **23** (both, Richard T. Nowitz); Getty Images pp. **8** (Brian Bailey), **22** (Stephen Alvarez); Superstock pp. **9** (age footstock); **16** (SuperStock, Inc.).

Cover photograph of the stalagmites in Carlsbad Caverns' Big Room reproduced with permission of Corbis/George H. H. Huey. Backcover image of a sandstone cave reproduced with permission of Corbis/David Muench.

Every effort has been made to contact copyright holders of any material reproduced in this book. Any omissions will be rectified in subsequent printings if notice is given to the publishers.

Contents

Landforms 4

What is a cave? 6

Features of a cave 12

Types of cave 14

What lives in a cave? 18

Visiting caves 20

Cave facts 22

Picture glossary 23

Index 24

Landforms

The land is made of different shapes.
These shapes are called landforms.

cave

A cave is a landform.
Caves are found all over the world.

What is a cave?

A cave is a large hole in the earth.

Caves are made of rock.
Caves are very dark.

Some caves are under the ground.

Some caves are in the sides of hills.

Some caves are big.
They are as big as a tall building.

Some caves are small.
You have to crawl to climb
inside the cave.

Features of a cave

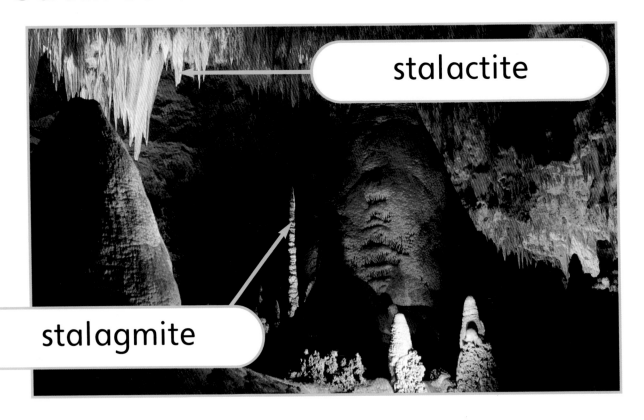

stalactite

stalagmite

Caves can have stalagmites growing up from the floor. They can also have stalactites growing down from the roof.

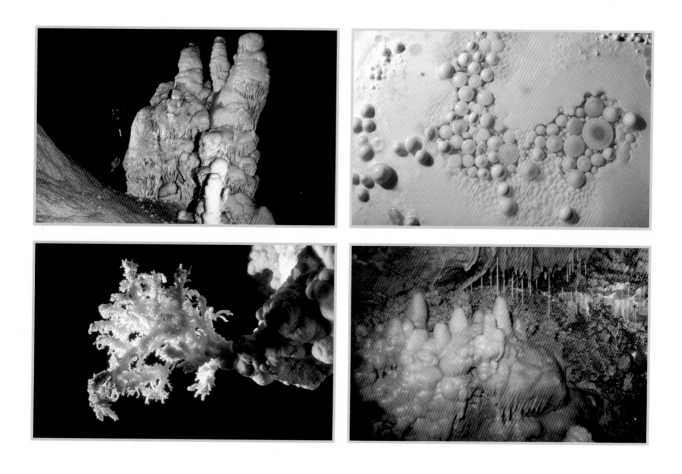

Stalagmites and stalactites come in many different shapes and sizes.

Types of cave

Some caves are by the sea.
The waves wear away the rock.
This forms the cave.

Some caves are made of ice.

Most caves are made of rock.
The entrance to a cave is called
a mouth.

This cave is made of sand. Millions of years ago the sand was pressed together and became as hard as rock.

What lives in a cave?

bat

Plants and animals live in caves.
Bats may hang from the roof of a cave.

Some people also live in caves.
They make their homes inside the
caves where it is cool.

Visiting caves

People like to visit caves.
Some people like to explore
deep inside a cave.

Caves are exciting places deep inside the Earth.

Cave facts

Mammoth Cave is in Kentucky, USA. It is the largest group of caves in the world.

Some cave animals are blind. These animals have a good sense of touch.

Picture glossary

stalactite a stony spike hanging like an icicle from the roof of a cave

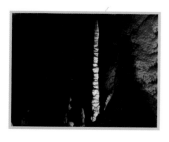

stalagmite a stony spike standing like a pillar on the floor of a cave

Index

ice 15

sand 17

sea 14

stalactite 12, 13, 23

stalagmite 12, 23

Notes to parents and teachers

Before reading

Talk about caves. Explain that they are landforms which are found underground or in the sides of hills or mountains. Explain that many caves are formed because water wears away the land and rock. Talk about stalactites and stalagmites. Explain that they are formed when water and minerals drip from the roofs of caves. Stalactites have pointed tips and stalagmites are rounded at the top.

After reading

Make a cave by spreading a length of dark fabric over a table. Encourage the children to individually crawl inside and experience the dark. Ask them to describe what it felt like. Draw bat shapes on black card and cut them out. Tell the children to mark the veins on the wings, the eyes, and the ears with white pencils. Hang the bats inside the "cave". Listen to a recording of "Fingal's Cave" by Mendelssohn. Discuss with the children how to move to the music to represent the sea as it swirls in and out of the cave.

Titles in the *Landforms* series include:

Hardback   0 431 18230 2

Hardback   0 431 18233 7

Hardback   0 431 18231 0

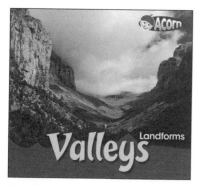

Hardback   0 431 18232 9

Hardback   0 431 18234 5

Find out about other titles from Heinemann Library on our website www.heinemann.co.uk/library